I0759502

This poem is dedicated to Strauss, the dog who saved me; my mother, Barb, who understood I needed him; and to all the dogs who have loved us more.

—JACKIE

What Do You Do When Your Dog Grows Old?

Published in 2026 by Red Comet Press, LLC, Brooklyn, NY

Library of Congress Control Number: 2024951522
ISBN (HB): 978-1-63655-171-5
ISBN (EBOOK): 978-1-63655-172-2

25 26 27 28 29 TLF 10 9 8 7 6 5 4 3 2 1

First Edition
Manufactured in China
Red Comet Press is distributed by ABRAMS, New York

RedCometPress.com

What Do You Do When Your Dog Grows Old?

A POEM BY JACKIE SHORT

ILLUSTRATIONS BY LUCY PICKETT

RED COMET PRESS • BROOKLYN

What do you
do when your dog
grows old?

When their feet
are tired and their
pads are worn.

When your words of
praise are hard to hear,
and their eyes are milky
from all of their years.

When their face
is changed and
turning gray.

What do you
do when your dog
grows old?

You Love them.

You rub the feet
that carried them
by your side.

You praise them
louder and harder;
you show them
your pride.

You guide them the way
they guided you,
and you never let them get
as lost as you once were.

SERVICE DOG

You kiss their nose
and hold their face.

And when it comes time
to put them to their final rest,
you do so knowing
you Loved them.

And they Loved you more.

They Loved you more.

A NOTE FROM THE AUTHOR

The way I write has always come from seeking catharsis and solace. My words are a release of tension. I wrote the original draft of this poem on a dinky phone while sitting in a pet store parking lot, waiting for a towing company to help with my car's dead battery.

Strauss, my service dog, was with me (as he always was), and I thought about how much time I had left with him. The urge to write struck me at that moment . . . so I did.

The road we traveled, side by side, for so many years had stretched on endlessly. I wrote this poem because I knew I would eventually have to walk it without him. I needed people to know he had been there. He kept me moving no matter how much I wanted to stop.

He keeps me moving now. I hope these same words keep you moving, too.